HOPE AND CHALLENGE

The Iranian President Speaks

Muhammad Khatami

Published by

Institute of Global Cultural Studies
Binghamton University
1997

Published by

Institute of Global Cultural Studies, *Binghamton University, State University of New York*, 1997

Library of Congress Cataloging-in-Publication Data

Muhammad Khatami,
Hope and Challenge: The Iranian President Speaks

1. Iranian Politics 2. Global Islam 3. Iran   4. Islamic Revolution

ISBN 1-883058-65-1

Announcement

The editors of this volume aim to introduce the English-speaking world to the perspectives of contemporary world leaders, as required by ever-increasing global interdependence. Institutions of higher learning have the obligation and privilege to present the views that shape the modern world. Academics are in a unique position to clarify such views without commercial concern or professional restrictions. In disseminating knowledge, academics fulfil their sacred responsibility to serve society. Plato recognized this dictum in his *Republic*, as did Nasser Khosrow in *Hermeneutic Openings and Spiritual Therapy (Goshayesh va Rahayesh)*. Both agree that knowledge is the essential ingredient of strength in a polity. There is no better way to know the visions of world leaders than to read their writings in clear translation. This publication expresses solely the positions of the author and does not necessarily reflect the views of the editors or home institutions.

Parviz Morewedge
Institute of Global Cultural Studies
Binghamton University

Kent P. Jackson
Religious Studies Center
Brigham Young University

Acknowledgments

The idea for this specific volume was conceived by Parviz Morewedge and Hossein Kamaly. The latter wrote the introduction and supervised the project. Kent P. Jackson guided the development and production of the text. The complex task of translation was aptly performed by Alidad Mafinezam, whose knowledge of Persian political discourse added much value to this volume. Recognition is also due to Amir-Hossein Zamaninia, who provided much-appreciated editorial advice on the first chapter and to Mohammad Aghajani-Memar for facilitating communication between the two sides of the Atlantic. Finally, the editors wish to express their gratitude to their home institutions, the *Institute of Global Cultural Studies* at Binghamton University, the State University of New York, and the *Religious Studies Center* at Brigham Young University.

Parviz Morewedge
Kent P. Jackson

Translator's Note

Every translation is at the same time an interpretation. . . . Where a translation is necessary, the gap between the spirit of the original words and that of their reproduction must be taken into account. It is a gap that can never be completely closed . . . the translation of a text . . . is necessarily a re-creation of the text guided by the way the translator understands what it says. The requirement that a translation be faithful cannot remove the fundamental gulf between the two languages. . . . A translator must understand that highlighting is a part of his task. . . . He must show his colors.

Hans-Georg Gadamer, *Truth and Method*

In translating President Muhammad Khatami's words from the Persian, I have focused on conveying the meaning and context of his discourse. While most of what follows can be viewed as a verbatim translation of the Persian original, in some instances paragraph and sentence structure have been modified for conceptual clarity. The syntactical differences between English and Persian have necessitated this move.

The correspondence between the vocabularies of the two languages is also imperfect. For example, the Persian word "azadi" could be translated as "freedom" or as "liberty." While these two words have different meanings in English, Persian does not distinguish between them. Nor does the Persian language make a distinction between the English words "modern" and "new." The corresponding word for both is "jadid." In such cases, I have chosen words and made minor modifications to convey my interpretation of the author's intent. On a stylistic note, unlike English, the third person singular pronoun in Persian is gender-neutral. I have thus alternated between "he" and "she" in the text.

Acknowledgment is due to Hossein Kamaly for entrusting me with this task. I am deeply indebted to Richard W. Bulliet who has provided much-needed intellectual guidance and logistical support.

Alidad Mafinezam
New York

HOPE AND CHALLENGE

The Iranian President Speaks

Muhammad Khatami

Table of Contents

Introduction

The landslide victory of Seyyed Muhammad Khatami in the May 23, 1997 presidential elections of the Islamic Republic of Iran has attracted substantial attention across the world. Ninety percent of all eligible voters, some 30 million Iranian women and men above the age of fifteen, participated in the elections. This is a sobering reminder of the capability of a people in deciding their own destiny. The election result has kindled hope in Iran and around the globe for a brighter and more harmonious future for Iranians. Still, formidable challenges face the new administration in political, economic and cultural arenas.

In our frantic world of media sensationalism, foundational and philosophical issues are rarely covered. Bombastic generalizations and naive stereotypes may suit the short-term agenda, but only at the expense of much-needed cross-cultural understanding. Having attracted over two-thirds of Iranian voters, President Khatami's message merits a fair hearing. In this spirit, together with Parviz Morewedge of Binghamton University, State University of New York, we decided to put into print a balanced collection of cultural and political essays and addresses by the new president of the Islamic Republic of Iran. We hope that this book can provide a clear and authentic view of some topical issues in Iran and the Islamic world.

The first two articles here are taken from President Khatami's collection of essays, *Bim-e mowj (Fear of the Wave)*, Sima-ye Javan, Tehran, 1993, pp. 129–68 and pp. 169–205. The third article is the text of an address delivered in Tehran at an international conference on information science sponsored by the National Library of Iran in the autumn of 1995. The English translation of President Khatami's inaugural address was obtained from *http://netiran.com*. Excerpts from his addresses are courtesy of the electronic library of the Gulf/2000 project at Columbia University. I wish to extend my gratitude to administrators of these informative resources, and to all those mentioned in the acknowledgments.

Hossein Kamaly
New York

CHAPTER ONE

Our Revolution and the Future of Islam

Civilizations rise and fall. From the dawn of history this has been the fate of Sumerian, Chaldean, Assyrian, Chinese, Indian, Persian, Greek, Roman and Islamic civilizations. At its zenith, Islam acted as the conduit between these ancient civilizations and the modern age. Today, it is Western civilization that reigns supreme, casting its shadow upon all corners of the world.

The Interplay of Civilizations

Unless they are completely unaware of each other's existence, civilizations ordinarily affect and transform one another. For instance, America's indigenous civilization was completely unknown to the outside world until Europeans discovered the continent. But once the connection was made, the massive tide of explorers and immigrants who conquered and appropriated the new world could not be held back. Using their superior power and resources, the newcomers ruthlessly subjugated and destroyed the continent's old civilization. The wave of European immigrants that took over the Americas eventually succeeded in turning North America into the most powerful center of Western civilization.

The give-and-take among civilizations is the norm of history. Prior to the discovery of the Americas, the civilizations of Asia, Africa, and Europe had been in contact since antiquity, transforming one another in various ways. Fundamentally influenced by Greek civilization, Islam played a central mediating role by introducing Europeans to the achievements of Greek thought and philosophy. Thus "new" civilizations are never new in the true sense, for they always feed on the work of previous civilizations, appropriating and digesting all that fits their needs, dispensing with all that does not.

The Main Sources of the Emergence of Civilizations

Of the many factors that spur the emergence, rise and demise of civilizations, two are fundamental: the dynamism of the human mind and the concomitant surfacing of new needs and necessities in human life.

The human mind is instinctively active, perpetually driven by a burning curiosity that confronts a never-ending chain of new questions to which it must find answers, or it will not rest or be content. But once a discovery is made, the new answers bring to view an untested world replete with new questions, an eternal cyclical process.

At the same time, humans strive to fulfill their material needs, which beckons them to seek greater mastery over the natural world through invention and innovation. The combination of the will to dominate nature and the will to creativity alters the material and psychological makeup of the human world, and this creates new needs and necessities.

The dynamism of the human constitution and the resulting search for answers to pressing questions or needs spurs a constant transformation of the human historical consciousness. And the same two fundamental qualities of humans that underpin the inevitability of change are also the cause of the emergence and decline of civilizations. While other human, social and natural factors slow down or accelerate the coming, going and interchange of civilizations, the desire and need for change is the most important in this regard.

Every civilization is based on a specific worldview which is itself shaped by a people's idiosyncratic historical experience. For as long as the existing worldview successfully addresses the fundamental questions and needs of a community, it remains in tact. But when the collective consciousness and soul of a people outgrows the limitations of the existing civilization, the search for new ideas begins in earnest, often taking the form of turning to other civilizations for clues. This is the secret of the emergence, flourishing and fall of all civilizations.

The Crisis of Civilizations

When it is first born and subsequently at the point of its demise, each civilization places its adherents in a state of crisis. At first, when a new covenant arises in the history of a people and the ground is ripe for the emergence of a new civilization, the social fabric is strained. The new civilization heralds new and often revolutionary customs and mores. But the previous civilization will not easily relinquish its entrenched and institutionalized dominance. Historically shaped social habits are hard to break. Much of society remains glued to the mental and emotional predilections of the previous era. The need to throw out the deeply ingrained attachments and replace them with a new worldview induces a painful identity crisis.

At the same time, the new civilization has not been tried out in real life. Its inner contradictions are hidden from view, for it has not passed the litmus test of experience. To endure and lay roots, the new civilization must adapt and fine-tune itself as it encounters the evolving realities of social life. Until this process of adaptation and transformation reaches its fruition, social identity crisis is the norm.

The other instance of crisis, at the point of the demise of a civilization, appears when the dominant worldview cannot satisfy the psychological, material, and social needs of its constituents. People begin to experience a troubling void and sterility. Again, the historically conditioned predilections that are rendered anachronistic will not be easily abandoned. This state of limbo can merely offer the veneer of civilization bereft of substance and soul. An existential void sets in that brings on a full-blown identity crisis.[1]

---

[1] This argument does not imply that each of the two types of crisis necessarily follows the other. Because of the connection of the "death crisis" of the first civilization to the "birth crisis" of the second, they must not be viewed as being identical, because:

First, my focus is on the crisis that one civilization creates, one at the peak of civilization and the other at its nadir, not the crisis of the end of one and the birth of the second. Second, even if the crisis of the end of one civilization and the crisis of the birth of another civilization mean the same thing, this mere connection does not mean that the we

The brief discussion above is meant to set up the fundamental question, what historical condition does our own society live in and what is going to become of it?

Crisis in the West

As noted above, ours is the age of the dominance and entrenchment of Western civilization, a civilization that has lived for more than four centuries and has made great strides in science, politics, and social regulation. But we must accept that the West today faces an acute crisis, a crisis in its thought and all other spheres. Those familiar with the history of Western civilization and its philosophical, scientific, and artistic expressions can more or less see the signs of this crisis. The West was not confronted with a crisis of this magnitude in the eighteenth and part of the nineteenth century. What does the current crisis signify?

---

should see them as the being one and the same, for these two crises are qualitatively different in nature, similar to the way life and death are different. Third, it is not as though as soon as a civilization dies there is immediately another one to replace it. Instead, a civilization comes, stays for centuries and then leaves. Different societies provide different breeding grounds for civilizations. To know this for certain requires greater and more careful scrutiny which this author has not had the chance to undertake. Nonetheless, we should not doubt the qualitative difference between these two kinds of crisis.

It is possible to assert that Western civilization is worn out and senile. Four centuries is a long time for a civilization — even though it is possible that in the past some civilizations may have lived longer than this. But science, technology and electronic communication have vastly accelerated the pace of change like never before. The life of Western civilization from the Renaissance to today cannot be viewed as short, and to treat Western civilization as old would not be an exaggeration.

From Crisis to Demise of the West?

This is not an easy question to take on. Crises are sometimes limited and temporary. This has often occurred in the life of civilizations which have had the capability to successfully confront crises and remain intact. Indeed, in the nineteenth century, the West managed to successfully surmount the crisis that it encountered.

The capitalist order, which represents the key feature of Western civilization, encountered great difficulties in the second half of the nineteenth century and during the two world wars of the first half of the twentieth century. But Marxism came to its rescue. The West managed to modify its mental and material structures, coming out of these crises in one piece.

Despite the claims of its protagonists, Marxism was an impractical and unrealistic philosophy. And precisely because of these deficiencies and its lack of adaptability, it did not last. It was kept standing for seventy years only through the use of force and propaganda. Still, although Marx did not offer a solid and comprehensive philosophy, he was a great pathologist of the capitalist order. What Marxists proposed forced the West to become introspective and to search for ways of adjusting capitalism's methods to the demands of the time, and to modify its social, economic and political order from within. One key tactic of the West was to replace its old colonialism — which was sowing the seeds of a worldwide explosion — with neocolonialism. This allowed the West to contain and diffuse the crisis, postponing its reemergence for a while.

But what about the present crisis? Can the West also pass through this difficult period unscathed? We cannot predict this with certainty, but to the extent that human understanding and research allows, we can collect evidence and observe empirical reality and arrive at a theory on that basis. This is an important task for objective and judicious academic research.

The West's Antidotes for Crisis

The West has adopted a strategy similar to the one it used at the beginning of this century which allowed it to circumvent previous crises: by modifying the ways of old colonialism into a more sophisticated neocolonialism. The so-called "new world order" is the West's new strategy for handling a crisis that has shaken it at the core.

Presenting itself as the main sponsor and protector of the "new world order," the United States is focused on adapting neocolonialism to the new age. The logic of this transformation is similar to the shift from old colonialism to neocolonialism.[2] There is other evidence attesting to the decline of the current Western civilization as well. While it is certain that Western civilization is old and worn out, the question of whether it has reached the end of its path needs more thinking and scrutiny. What does the future hold?

Crisis in Our Revolutionary Society

Our society also confronts a crisis today, and although this crisis is to some extent attributable to global conditions, it is different from the West's crisis. Through our revolution we tried to free ourselves from the shackles of the West's

---

[2] The very quest for a "new world order" is an obvious sign that the current order is under serious strain as it fails to meet people's fundamental needs. The ever-more frequent and extensive discussion of the "new" order, especially in the West, is itself proof for the existence of a crisis in the West and in the rest of the world. We cannot overlook the fact that oppressive powers, led by the United States, continue their deceitful attempt to manipulate the current historical moment and world consciousness to assert their destructive domination of the developing world under the guise of the "new world order." This is an attempt to subvert and prevent fundamental transformations in the current order that would benefit all of humanity. There is voluminous material on the "new world order" which I defer to another occasion.

domination. Our revolution made us introspective, we decided to struggle for our independence, to be masters of our own fate. In this regard, we have made great headway in the political, economic and cultural spheres. But is it possible that we fall into the West's trap of domination again? This depends on the path we choose in the future and on what the West's own destiny is. The Islamic revolution was a momentous event in the history of the Iranian nation and the Islamic community, and we can rightly say that because of our revolution we have dispensed with borrowed and Western values that dominated our thinking. And through realizing our own authentic historical and cultural identity, we have laid a completely new groundwork for regulating our society.

Our revolution proposed the creation of a religiously based system and our society accepted this with enthusiasm and gallantly took steps to reach this great goal. The crisis that we experience today can only be remedied if we shed the vestiges of our borrowed identity and don a new garb. Our current crisis is the crisis of birth which I referred to earlier. Our new civilization is on the verge of emergence.

We cannot confront this crisis with trepidation. We must embrace it boldly and intelligently. Only when we have understood the most fundamental historical questions of this epoch can we develop the willingness to solve them.

We wish to base our life on the tenets of Islam; we possess the will to create an Islamic civilization. At a time when modern civilization is going through its last days, or at least experiencing senility, we must ask, didn't Islamic civilization already emerge once and end centuries ago? And doesn't the death of a civilization mean that we can no longer base thought and action on its teachings? Doesn't this rule apply to our history? Does the coming and passing of Islamic civilization mean that the period of Islam, which provided the basis for Islamic civilization, is over?

If the answer to this question is affirmative, has our revolution been a fruitless effort moving against the traditions of creation and laws that govern the march of civilizations? This is one of the most important and pressing questions that confronts our revolution. If we do not approach it with level-headedness and objectivity, if we cannot find a solid answer to this question, our revolution will inevitably encounter great danger and difficulty.

My answer to the above question is negative. But with this answer I do not want to debunk the rule that I proposed about civilizations. Generally, I believe that the law holds, but on the basis of my view of religion, I take this case not as a falsifier of the above but as falling outside its purview. For what creates a civilization is the vision and effort of humans, while religion is above and beyond the vision of individuals and societies and thus transcends civilizations.

If the sun has set on Islamic civilization despite its many monumental achievements, a certain view of religion — which was appropriate for that period — has ended, not the age of religion itself.

One of the greatest difficulties that religions have historically encountered has arisen out of confusing the specific religious teachings designed for specific times and places with the idea of religion itself. Naturally, with the obsolescence of age- and place-specific religious thought, some have the impression that the era of religion in over as well. But religion transcends the specific civilizations that it gives rise to.

Civilization addresses specific needs and dilemmas of a community in a particular time and place. When conditions and times change, new questions arise that in turn require new answers— and hence a new civilization.

Religion, on the other hand, sheds light on questions of eternity, charting a general and timeless path for humanity, giving direction to life despite its ever-changing circumstances. Religion guides human talents to their plateau, instilling in people a sense of duty in different historical conditions.

Thus if we think of religion as being identical to civilization or culture, then the passing of civilization must imply that the era of religion is over as well. But if we believe that religion supersedes and transcends civilization and the specific mores of community, then religion can contain many different interpretations that give rise to various civilizations. The inevitable transformations of human life will do no damage to the eternal life of religion.

In this view, the core of religion possesses such dynamism that in any age it can provide answers to questions and a fulfillment of needs. Thus, while the old Islamic civilization has vanished, religion stands deeply rooted and can generate new civilizations, even though the specific interpretations of religion which have spawned past Islamic civilizations, have withered.

With this general picture, I will try to address a number of pressing issues that confront our society today.

Our vision of consolidating a system of religious governance in our future-oriented society cannot be materialized in a vacuum. We cannot implement this vision without full contact with the international community. We have come upon this important task at a time when Western civilization dominates the world. Yet, simultaneously, we must try to free ourselves from the domination of the West. It is thus natural that we confront the West, and the upshot of this confrontation will determine our future.

Two Countenances of the West

The West displays two features: one political, the other intellectual. Its political orientation serves as the most outward manifestation or veneer of Western civilization. The intellectual foundations of Western civilization illustrate its general worldview. We must diligently distinguish between these two aspects. Only then can we find the proper way of confronting the West. This path must be traveled with prudence.

Even though the West has gotten old, it maintains tremendous political, economic, military, social, and technological power, simultaneously wielding a formidable propaganda and communication apparatus to manage the world's perceptions. Equally important, the global economy is controlled and regulated by Western financial institutions.

The West's advanced systems and institutions often legitimize its political power, ensuring its decisive presence in all significant global developments. The military might of Western capitalism is also vast, and even if we concede that official military pacts are not as common as they were, the military and destructive power of the West remains intact.

Politically, the West aims to govern all comers of the world and to dominate the theory and practice of international relations. It possesses the material and symbolic sources of power simultaneously, and it will stop at nothing to achieve its goals and protect its interests. Our struggle with the West is of life-and-death importance.

In its political embodiment, the West does not wish us — or any people — to be independent, free, and masters of our own fate. For if one feature of Western imperialism is violating others' territories and exploiting their economies, the concomitant feature is dominating the world of ideas. The West propagates a worldview that lures its preys into subjugation.

We confront a determined enemy that brings all of its material, military, and informational resources to convince us to surrender, or risk being destroyed if we resist. The bitter experience of the confrontation between domination-seeking powers and the oppressed masses is too evident to be hidden to anyone.

In political confrontations, the enemy uses the mask of science and culture to deceive us. But in reality its only wish is to induce a people to surrender to its wishes and serve its interests, and to appropriate all of the victims' resources to serve the imperialist power.

Although the West has no qualms about using the most repressive and violent techniques, even its military and overtly oppressive measures are shrouded in seemingly humanistic and misleading guises that divert public opinion from reality.

When colonial powers violate other peoples, they never concede that their aim is to rob the victims' resources or to politically subjugate them. Instead, by abusing their persuasive powers they try to disguise their crimes through words and ideas that are acceptable to all of humanity. From old times, colonial powers have used the excuse of developing and civilizing other peoples to violate them and rape their lands. Today, like before, the political motto of the West remains defending freedom, human rights, and democracy.

At this juncture, our struggle against the West is central to our survival. Any form of reconciliation and appeasement, given the penchant of the opponent for deception, will lead to nothing but our debasement and trampling on our pride. We must struggle against this with all our might, and victory is not beyond our reach. We must depend on God and ask for His guidance, relying on our own historical identity which we have regained through our revolution. With faith in the power of an awakened people and by strengthening the desire for independence and freedom, we must stand firmly opposed to an enemy that lacks humanitarian incentives. This is indeed possible. The awesome resistance of our nation to the conspiracies and crimes of the oppressors can be a lesson for all nations who wish to regain their independence and pride.

Yet, while ignoring the politically treacherous goals and conspiracies of the West can be catastrophic, we cannot see the West merely in political terms or reduce its whole civilization to political issues. This would also lead us to a harmful dead end.

Western civilization is not limited to its political aspects. Alongside Western politics, there is a system of values and thinking which we must also come to understand and learn to deal with. Here we are confronted with our philosophical and moral opposite, not just with a political rival. To understand the West, the best tool is rationality, not heated, flag-waving emotionalism. Not just here, but nowhere can force offer an effective response to a way of thinking that we consider flawed. That would be self-defeating and counterproductive.

However, mired as they are in shallowness and hype, it is possible that opportunists will take any thought and cul-

ture that their audience dislikes and give it political salience
and introduce it as a conspiracy to destroy their political base.
This does not come from contemplation but from the need to
justify their irrational encounter with opposite views, obviat-
ing the need for education and a more powerful logic. This is
very common among the overly politicized.

Resorting to force is appropriate in confronting a military invasion, conspiracy, or political sabotage. But the way
to oppose thought and culture is not through the use of military, security and judicial means, for using force only adds
fuel to the opposite side's fire. We must confront the thought
of the opponent by relying on rationality and enlightenment
and through offering more powerful and compelling counter
arguments. Only comprehensive and attractive thinking can
repel this sort of danger. If we do not possess such logic and
knowledge, we must endeavor to attain it as our first priority.
Islam furnishes us with such a logic and thought. And if some
Muslims are devoid of it, the fault lies with them — not with
Islam.

If, God forbid, some people want to impose their rigid
thinking on Islam and call it God's religion — since they lack
the intellectual power to confront the opposite side's thinking
on its own terms — they resort to fanaticism. This merely
harms Islam, without achieving the aims of those people.

In rejecting the West, we wish to free ourselves from
its political, mental, cultural, and economic domination, for
as Muslims we differ from them fundamentally in worldview
and values. Thus, to understand our points of contention and

for negating the rival's domination, we have no choice but to precisely and objectively appraise and understand the West.

We have to keep in mind that Western civilization rests on the idea of "liberty" or "freedom." These are indeed the most cherished values for humanity in all ages, and to be fair, Western civilization's march from the Middle Ages to modern centuries has broken many superstitions and chains in thought, politics and society. The West has indeed freed humans from the shackles of many oppressive traditions. It has successfully cast aside the deification of regressive thinking that had been imposed on the masses in the name of religion. It has also broken down subjugation to autocratic rule. These are all positive steps and adaptive to the traditions of creation. Yet, at the same time, the view of the West about humans and freedom has been rigid and one-dimensional, and this continues to take a heavy toll on humanity.

When confronting the opponent in the name of rejecting the West and defending religion, if we step on freedom we will have caused a great catastrophe. Neither the traditions of creation allow this nor does Islam desire it. But if rejecting the West means critiquing its view of freedom, humanity, and the world, then we will have achieved our most fundamental historical mission.

Indeed, we take issue with the West on the notion of freedom. We do not think that the Western definition of freedom is complete. Nor can the Western view of freedom guarantee human happiness. The West is so self-absorbed in its historical setting and thoughts that it cannot see the calamities that its incorrect view of humanity and freedom has caused. If we look at the West from the outside, we can objectively judge this issue. But achieving this important task requires much intellectual rigor and knowledge.

Benefiting from the West's Experience

As Western civilization becomes increasingly worn out and senile, humanity is today searching for a new vision for its future, awaiting a new civilization which is more capable of meeting its material and spiritual needs and wants. Through our Islamic revolution, we have endeavored to create a new system whose values and visions differ markedly from what is prevalent in the Western-dominated world. Can we claim that our Islamic revolution has opened a new chapter in human history?

As noted above, no civilization is independent of the influences of those that have preceded it. The nature of the human mind does not allow it to suddenly and completely dispense with the experiences and knowledge of previous times. The secret of the evolution of human life on planet earth is that every person and generation starts its movement where others have left off. If all generations started and ended at the same point, human destiny would be no different from that of bees. The difference between humans and other social animals is that humans learn from their past experience, improve upon it, and leave their achievements for the next generation. And this process has continued uninterrupted for as long there has been a human race. Thus, there is no limit to human evolution.

Civilization, which is the fruit of humans' intellectual, emotional and practical endeavors, works the same way. A vibrant, civilization-building thought is a thought that incorporates all the positive aspects of the previous civilizations, digests it and adds to it.

Now, on the basis of our popular revolution we wish to construct an Islamic system. But we can only think of our revolution as giving rise to a new civilization if we have the ability to absorb the positive aspects of Western civilization and the wisdom to recognize the negative aspects of it and to refrain from absorbing them. This means that if we can break through the dead ends that the West has reached because of its values, and pass through them unscathed, we will succeed in our mission.

If we must adopt the positive features of Western civilization, simultaneously casting aside its deficiencies, we have no choice but to correctly and comprehensively understand the West in the first place. We must judge it fairly and objectively and learn from and use its strengths, staying clear of its defects by relying on our revolution's Islamic values. And it is obvious that this approach is different from a rigidly political appraisal of the West. Those who cannot separate the political West from the nonpolitical West are acting against the interests of the nation and the Islamic revolution, even though they may be doing so inadvertently. Here, introspection, rationality and objectivity will be effective, not harsh words and violence.

The Difficulties of Our Revolution

In all fairness, our Islamic revolution has been the source of great transformations in many corners of the world, and we, as the source of revolution, are naturally the most affected by these transformations. In the wake of our revolution, we have a mission which is as grand and formidable as the challenges we encounter. Passing through this difficult stage requires much wisdom and farsightedness, as well as patience and perseverance.

Although Islam had existed for centuries in the collective consciousness of believers as a collection of thoughts and values, our revolution propelled it into the contemporary political and social sphere, where it stands steadfast against its opponents. At the same time, this development has brought three novel challenges to the fore: our people's expectations, the opponent's treachery and conspiracy, and discord within our society.

First, our people's expectations. Now that a new system based on new ideas has taken over the reins of governance, people expect a great deal from it. This is especially true of those who have sacrificed for the system. Before the Islamic revolution, people did not have many expectations because our economy, culture, politics and educational system were dominated by the enemy, giving us the sense that we were not masters of our own fate. But as an Islamic, independent government has come to power — as all of the state's resources have been placed in Islam's hands — people have the right to expect the fulfillment of their needs and wants.

People wish to know specifically how the new system will regulate their lives and guarantee their rights. They also want to know the system's policy toward science, technology, as well as social justice and equity.

At this juncture, people will not be satisfied with promises alone; they want real, tangible, and practical results. And our system will be successful only if it can meet these expectations.

Some expectations are undoubtedly unrealistic. No government can work miracles overnight and eradicate all bottlenecks. Nor have all of people's expectations been based on a realistic appraisal of available resources. It is conceivable that unrealistic visions as well as impractical and unattainable ideologies have spurred these exaggerated expectations. Still, government must have the power to satisfy people's needs and guide them to modify their expectations and views. If it is not possible to meet all expectations — and it is not — people have to at least be convinced that our orientation is generally toward a fulfilling life, focused on meeting their spiritual and material needs.

Our society has to believe that what the revolution has offered and what it expects of people will simultaneously meet individual and societal needs, utilizing all of society's human resources and achievements. Society must also believe that our system is not burdened with the shortcomings and strains that bedevil our opponents.

The natural expectations of people puts officials and the elite under great pressure to perform, and the enemy fans the flames of people's expectations in various ways.

Second, the opponent's treachery and conspiracy. Before the victory of our revolution, we had many theoretical disagreements with opposing schools of thought. Those confrontations were easy to carry out because there was no real friction. But when ideas are put into practice and taken to the social and political sphere, opponents feel more threatened and thus resort to more violent and comprehensive confrontation.

Conspiracy to overthrow the revolutionary system, spying, economic pressure, fomenting pessimism and dejection among our people, attributing all our problems to the system's officials and portraying them as incompetent in meeting people's difficulties, and even resorting to military force for damaging the revolution and its popular base, are among actions taken by opponents who see their interests threatened by the new system. Our great nation in this period has experienced all sorts of enemy conspiracies. Just when the system and its managers need people's calm and optimism more than ever to focus all their thoughts and ingenuity on meeting society's needs, we encounter a heavy storm of enmity and conspiracy that sometimes forces us to focus our resources on counteracting the danger posed by the foreign enemy and its domestic sympathizers.

These are among our greatest difficulties at this juncture. And there is no other way than to confront these realities. In the midst of these pressing difficulties, we must persevere and march on with patience, confidence and wisdom.

Third, discord within. In the last hundred years our society has experienced two acute woes which have weakened and undermined its fabric. These woes have become more chronic and troubling at this sensitive juncture in our history. One is secular intellectualism, the other being unenlightened religious dogma.

The Secular Intellectual

Our society has a religious, identity. All throughout Shiism's history the clergy have played a crucial role in awakening people to social pathologies, inciting them to fight injustice, awakening their religious identity. In our history, Islam has perpetually invited people to unity in religious belief, protecting their individual and social dignity. With their incessant calls to social justice throughout the history of Islam, populist religious leaders have served as society's most astute pathologists and healers.

That is why Muslim societies have never harbored a negative view of religion. This is in stark contrast to Western societies where unsavory and misguided religious leaders have turned people away from religion.

In the Muslim world, especially in Iran, whenever oppressed people have risen against tyranny, their activism has always been channeled through religion. People have always witnessed the fiery and bloodied face of religious revolutionaries who have risen to fight oppression and despotism.

Our social conscience is replete with memories of the clash of true believers with hypocrites who have used religion to justify people's misery. Our part of the world has witnessed the historical antagonism between truth and justice-seeking religion and the oppressive and misguided views of religion that have been the tool of oppressors.

Is it not true that in the history of Islam, religion has opposed religious and secular tyranny? Haven't most martyrs of truth been religious activists? Is it not the case that over the past hundred years religion has been the greatest champion of the fight against despotic agents of colonialism? Hasn't the experience of religious struggle, among other revolutionary and nationalist experiences — some of which are worthy of praise — been the most successful?

Our society is religious, and it is natural that secular intellectuals have never enjoyed a social base or a place in our people's hearts.

Unfortunately, what has been called intellectualism in our society has been a movement that has been superficial and cut off from the people. Never has the voice of self-appointed intellectuals traveled beyond the cafeterias and coffee houses where they have posed as a political opposition. Even if people have heard their voice, they have found it incomprehensible. Thus, there has never been any mutual understanding.

And if public-minded intellectualism came to the fore and gained respect, it was through people who cast their claims in authentic, traditional, and religious terms. This was the reason for the vast popularity of figures such as Jalal Al-e Ahmad[3] and Ali Shariati.[4] These two were real intellectuals, and our society felt that they were a part of the people and spoke to the people's pains and concerns.

The secular intellectual, knowingly or not, pours water into the enemy's mill, the same enemy who is against our independence, who opposes our people's authentic culture, religion, and freedom. And history testifies that this group has on the whole been on the same side as, and has sometimes actively cooperated with, despotic systems propped up by foreigners. But fortunately, because it lacks deep roots in our

---

[3] Translator's Note. Jalal Al-e Ahmad (1923–1969). Seminal and prolific Iranian writer who popularized the effects of the cultural imperialism of the West or "Westoxication" among his generation.

[4] Translator's Note. Ali Shariati (1923–1977). Iranian sociologist and reformer of religious thought who played an important role in bridging the gap between Islamic thought and modern Iranian intellectuals. His numerous books and speeches, widely disseminated before the 1979 revolution, were instrumental in arousing Islamic revolutionary sentiment among Iranians.

culture and people's souls, it has not had much effect. And today also I believe secular intellectuals present no real danger, even though they may foment chaos in the minds of the young and other susceptible parts of society. Still, they may provide a foothold and opening for the enemy to penetrate society.

Religious Dogma

The other main problem we face is the parochialism and regressive visions of the dogmatic. Religious dogma is nothing more than ascribing sanctity and eternity to the limited and incomplete interpretations of humans, and giving priority to emotions over rationality and realistic appraisal.

If we ask dogmatic believers — who may see themselves as thinkers and intellectuals — what they expect from the revolution, they claim that they want a return to Islamic civilization.

We must alert such people that their wishes are anachronistic. The specific thoughts that underpinned Islamic civilization ended with the passing of that civilization. If it had maintained its dynamism, relevance and ability to provide answers to people's problems, that civilization would have endured.

Dogma presents the most formidable obstacle for institutionalizing a system that wishes to provide a model for the present and future of human life, a system based on a more powerful logic than competing schools and ideologies.

The effect of dogma on our society which has a religious identity is vast. And its negative effect is greater than secularism, especially because the dogmatic usually project the aura of religious legitimacy. Their religious duties compel them to act but they have no connection to authentic Islam, the Islamic revolution, or to the present and the future.

Imam Khomeini,[5] especially in the last two years of his life, was deeply concerned with the danger that dogma and backward vision posed to the revolution's path and the progress and welfare of Islamic society. In line with all of Imam Khomeini's warnings, vigilance about this phenomenon is crucial to us and the future of the Islamic revolution.

The Void in Religious Intellectualism

Here, I want to touch on one of the most important deficiencies of our society at this sensitive juncture, hoping that it spurs debate among thinkers, irrespective of whether they accept my proposition or reject or modify it.

---

[5] Translator's Note. Ayatollah Rouhollah Khomeini (1902?–1989). Leader of the Iranian revolution of 1979 and the founder of the Islamic Republic of Iran.

In my view, the greatest defect we have in the sphere of thought and development is the lack or weakness of religious intellectualism, even though I see the ground as ripe for its emergence and growth.

An intellectual, in my view, is one who lives in his own time and understands the issues and problems confronting humanity in that period. He keenly pursues such knowledge, and because he understands the problems of the day, he represents the only hope for finding solutions to those problems. For how can we expect someone to solve a problem when he does not know that a problem exists? Here, moral rectitude will not suffice. Nor will knowledge by itself. A moral person who is a moving encyclopedia but lives outside his time, for whom the most pressing problems are for example the second and third Islamic centuries, cannot solve even the smallest of today's problems, for today's problems do not interest him. But unless one is aware of current questions and problems, one will not be able to solve them.

In contrast, the main quality of an intellectual is that she lives in her own time, taking on a social responsibility, her mind constantly curious and restive about reality and human destiny. An intellectual is one who respects rationality and thinking and also knows the value of freedom.[6]

---

[6] My interpretation of the intellectual is based on convention. I use this concept to refer to actual, existing individuals. Others may have interpretations that do not allow a combination of intellectu-

Who is a Religious Believer?

A believer is one whose vision of being transcends the small cage of the material, and while he sees humans as having come from nature, he does not see them as limited to the natural world. Instead he sees every human as bigger than the whole of nature, because nature is limited while humans are, in a way, limitless and eternal. Just as the questions and needs of humans know no limits, time and space cannot limit and circumscribe humans in their narrow bounds. And for this reason humans look at the future and at the past, and with the aid of their mental faculties break the bounds of nature to find the gateway to transcend it.

The religious intellectual is one who loves humanity, understands its problems, and feels a responsibility toward its destiny and respects human freedom. She feels that humans have a divine mission and wants freedom for them. Whatever blocks the path to human growth and evolution, she deems as being against freedom.

Our dynamic society at this sensitive juncture badly needs religious intellectuals. If religion and intellectualism are combined, we can hope that our great Islamic revolution will

---

alism and religious belief. But it is unwarranted to confine ourselves to the prejudiced interpretation of a certain social group.

be the harbinger of a new era in human history. But if these two are separated, each will endanger the health of society.

When you mention God to secular intellectuals, they say they prefer to focus on humans. When you mention humans to the dogmatically religious, they say they prefer God. But the religious intellectual seeks "Godly humans," a creation whose emergence is as pressing a need today as it will always be.

I hope that through our revolution and a well-conceived connection between these two spheres — by connecting religious seminaries and the main centers of thinking in today's world, meaning universities — we will witness the emergence of the religious intellectual. This is a scenario that has neither the deficiencies of secular intellectualism nor those of dogmatic religious belief. Such a movement must shoulder the grand mission of our revolution and solve the crisis that is born out of the birth of a new system, all to benefit humanity, moving us toward a future replete with fulfillment and growth.

CHAPTER TWO

Fears and Hopes

Even those opposed to our revolution's goals and ideals concede its greatness. Unprecedented conspiracies and planning against us offer ample proof that this revolution has been taken seriously, its greatness indisputable even to its enemies. The Islamic revolution has spread its momentum across the Muslim world and beyond. It has given new hope to Muslims and downtrodden peoples who seek freedom and justice, hence affecting the world's intellectual and political climate.

This sort of transformation cannot help but create friction and anxiety in the society that originated it. Thus, our society's post-revolutionary anxiety results from the flux we are going through as we enter a new phase in our history. But this should be no cause for worry.

At the same time, proportional to its extent and seriousness, the fears and hopes that this transformation has given rise to are great as well: fear of all that threatens the revolution and hope for the bright, fulfilling future of revolutionary society.

Thus, we expect thinkers to know not only the pillars of the revolution but also the problems that it encounters. Thinkers must focus on the relationship of the revolution to current realities in the world. Only in this way can we preserve all that is true and just, changing what is not.

In my mind, the primary challenge confronting our revolution is the fundamental opposition or schism of its pillars to what is prevalent in today's world. The intellectual foundations and goals of our revolution are at odds with most

globally dominant values, sometimes negating them alto-
gether. This is only natural because every revolution opposes
the current order, having arisen precisely for this purpose in
the first place. But in our case, this opposition is particularly
intense because of the power our opponent wields in the
world of ideas.

The world opposed to our revolution possesses a ma-
ture, well-thought-out intellectual and political system that
has been centuries in the making, fine-tuned by generations of
seminal scientists and thinkers. A centuries-long tradition of
invention and innovation has developed into a solid socio-
political system whose main ammunition is the title it has to a
deeply entrenched value system. Its political and philosophical vision commands a large, global audience and is backed by
capable scientists and experts.

Our opponent also commands an awesome economic,
political, and military power, more diverse and complex than
anything we have seen in the past. But this should not intimi-
date us because great revolutions have come face to face with
powerful intellectual and political systems in the past and succeeded in transforming them. We who claim that our revolution is great cannot be overwhelmed by the power and size of
the revolution's opponents.

What makes our predicament even more challenging,
however, is that the West's intellectual, moral, and political
system, as portrayed and propagated today, is attuned and
adaptive to basic human nature. People are naturally drawn
to it.

The champions of modern thought and civilization claim that their vision rests on "freedom," a claim that we must take seriously, especially now that socialist thought has been wiped away with the demise of the Soviet camp. This has been taken to mean that a system based on Western notions of freedom is the only one that can endure.

The opponent of the Islamic revolution relies on the principle of "freedom" and derives much of its power from this because freedom represents a central, instinctive human goal. When freedom is depicted as allowing people to do whatever they desire, this depiction matches the strong human urge to live free of limitations. But in practice limitless freedom is not possible, and "freedom," the way the West defines it, is reducible to license or being free of the encroachment of others. Thus, the yardstick here is the thought and will of humans, meaning that the majority must decide what the limits of liberty are and make laws and regulations on that basis.

Champions of modern values believe that no obstacles should be placed in the way of people that would prevent them from doing whatever they desire — unless these wishes conflict with the wishes of others. Although it must incorporate a series of human-designed restrictions, the system is in general agreeable with instinctive and basic human needs and desires which do not have to be learned. In other words, all of the physical, worldly inclinations that the current Western order satisfies are strong motivations in every human's life. No work or education is necessary to find these inclinations compelling, and a system that satisfies them seems highly attractive.

Our revolution, on the contrary, has called people to values whose attainment requires much will, effort and labor. We base our system on abstinence, honesty and rectitude, which are not inborn in human nature. And although humans have the talent to attain them, to achieve them they must labor over many difficulties and accept that paying moral dues requires much work.

Thus, the opponent of our revolution, while possessing much economic, political, military, scientific and technological power, puts forth a set of values that are agreeable with basic human needs and inclinations. This makes its system look as though it has a moral and utopian vision too.

The West claims that it not only allows humans to be free of restrictions on their behavior and instinctive wishes, but that such a life is morally superior to all other systems because the main goal of human life — the will to freedom — is fulfilled.

True, humans are attracted to nothing the way they are attracted to freedom, and they have arguably never sacrificed as much for the attainment of any goal as they have for freedom. Today, humans are offered a system that invites them to eat and drink as they like, dress and speak as they wish, and to think freely. Simultaneously, the goal of life in such a system is prosperity and power, both viewed as serving the greatest, holiest goal of humanity, namely freedom. Thus, the West uses the most basic and hence powerful human instincts to solidify its position. This is misleading because despite what it claims, the West is far from achieving true freedom. We want a system based on abstinence and high morality that only comes through relentless endeavor and the courage to embark upon moral and spiritual growth. This is true freedom, but people need to be taught to see it this way.

What further fans the flames of antagonism between us and our opponent today is the power and reach of global electronic communications. In our era each person is effortlessly in contact with others in all corners of the world. The borders and limits that separated societies in the past have vanished at the hands of new communication technologies that allow instantaneous transfer of information and news across continents. Our opponent also controls this vital resource, possessing the complex technical knowledge to mass-disseminate images and waves to the world community: an uncanny skill for public relations and manufacturing consent through sights and sounds using the most refined, complex, and effective methods of science and technology to win others over to its thoughts and lifestyle.

Ours is a time when no one can blind the individual mind to what goes on in the world. Everyone everywhere is defenselessly bombarded by a barrage of information on world events, guided by views that world powers want disseminated.

Our opponent does not tolerate societies that differ from it, seeking to nip all independent movements in the bud.

The West thinks of nothing but its own interests, and if a people turn away from its values or refuse to serve its interests, it focuses all of its vast capabilities to force them to surrender or risk annihilation. And this is precisely why our revolution has encountered waves of conspiracies and pressures from the moment it was born.

We must clarify the relationship of our revolution to the difficulties it meets abroad. But this should not make us ignore our own internal problems.

One of the most important difficulties we face is the separation of Islam from the practical demands of the social and political sphere. Now that our Islamic revolution wishes to institutionalize a new mode of individual and social life, as we encounter the world and its realities we suffer from a theoretical void. That is a void in our ability to regulate society and human relations through Islamic ideas that work. For centuries Islamic thought has been artificially relegated to the sidelines. Islam has not been allowed to govern and regulate social relations. Instead, society's reins have either been in the hands of anti-Islamic forces or controlled by groups who have merely used Islam for self-aggrandizement, propagating it solely to legitimize their power and rule.

Real Islam, during this long hiatus, turned into a force of opposition against corrupt and obsolete systems which ruled in its name. Today, our revolution yearns to build a system based on real Islam. Still, even our vision of real Islam encounters inadequacies when it attempts to address today's social problems.

We are fortunate that the relentless effort and struggle of courageous thinkers and clergy saved real Islam from falling prey to political vicissitudes by transferring knowledge of such an Islam to new generations, never letting it perish.

Islamic thought delves with unrivaled richness into matters that transcend time, space and material reality, shedding a profound light on issues above and beyond the workaday world. Islamic mysticism or *Erfan* is unique in the history of human thought. Compared to other systems of transcendental knowledge, *Erfan* is the best equipped to address supernatural phenomena. But today, as we wish to put Islam into practice and apply its teachings to the material social and political world, we encounter the above-noted intellectual void which can only be remedied if we rely on authentic Islamic sources, principles, and rules of conduct.

Our Islamic revolution's utopian visions were clearly articulated in the slogans that came to define our ideology in the early days of the revolution. These slogans either flowed directly from the minds of the people or were articulated by the aware, enlightened leadership and subsequently embraced by the masses.

Our goals may seem beyond reach at the moment. A value system is only as strong and durable as the realistic and practical affirmation of its tenets. It cannot exist in the realm of thought and imagination alone. To get to our ideal in an un-ideal world, we must achieve an appropriate balance among order, welfare, and pace in our society. If the rhythms of our society do not meet the demands of the times we live in, it is only natural that we encounter puzzles and difficulties. It is precisely here that we need a mental breakthrough. Arriving at a practical, workable system attuned also to the demands of the revolution must be given the highest priority.

Our society's fabric is strained by vice; economic and political difficulties loom large, and we suffer from the diluted identity of Westoxication — neither ourselves, nor Western. But if the root of the problem is to be found elsewhere, and we can solve the problem at its root, we will succeed in overcoming other difficulties more quickly, with greater confidence and effect.

In practical matters, as we have depended on theology to give order to the individual and social world, we face serious inadequacies. This can only mean that our theology must evolve to meet the demands of the revolution and also the practical needs we have today. Here we can turn to the grand leader of the revolution, Imam Khomeini, who was a visionary Muslim leader, philosopher, theologian, and mystic. We turn to him to uncover the void and inadequacies we must overcome to achieve our goals:

> We must bring about the realization of the practical laws of Islam, undeterred by the deceitful West, the invasive East and their globally dominant modes of diplomacy. For as long as theology is trapped in the books and in the clergy's chests, there is no harm done to world devourers. And until the clergy are active in every sphere, they will not realize that religious authority and knowledge not enough. Centers of religious

education and the clergy must be abreast of the times and have the pulse of the present in their hands and know the needs of the future. Always a few step ahead of events, they must come up with effective responses. Our current methods of running our society are likely to change in the years ahead. And human society may come to utilize the issues facing Islam.

> Khomeini, Rouhollah (Imam), *Sahifey-e Noor* (The Book of Light). Volume 21, page 100.

We all agree that the Imam soared at the peak of religious-mystical awareness. The yearning of the revolution for truth and justice blossomed under his leadership. Based on the Imam's thinking, a cleric who is unaware of the demands of his time, and lives with ideas that are hundreds of years old, will not be able to relieve society from today's strains however noble his intentions might be. As well as understanding today's demands he must have the pulse, thoughts and needs of the future in his hands, so he can shape events instead of being at their mercy. The Imam says in another place:

In Islamic government, there should always be room for revision. Our revolutionary system demands that various, even opposing viewpoints be allowed to surface. No one has the right to restrict this. It is crucial to understand the demands of society and governance such that Islamic government can make policies that benefit Muslims. Unity in method and practice is essential. It is here that traditional religious leadership prevalent in our seminaries will not suffice. Ibid, page 47.

And,

> One of the greatest problems of religious leadership is
> the role of time and place in decision making. Govern-
> ment specifies a practical philosophy for dealing with
> sacrilege and internal and external difficulties. But these
> problems can not only not be solved by a purely theo-
> retical view of religion but will lead us to dead ends and
> the appearance that constitutional laws have been
> breached. While you must ensure that religious infrac-
> tions do not happen — and I hope God doesn't bring
> that day — you must focus all your effort on ensuring
> that when encountering military, social and political is-
> sues, Islam does not seem to lack practical utility.
>
> Ibid, page 61.

And on another occasion,

> But on the question of the educational methods and re-
> search in religious schools, I believe in traditional theol-
> ogy and deem straying from it to be inappropriate. Re-
> ligious leadership is proper and correct only in this way.
> But this does not mean that Islamic theology is not dy-
> namic. Time and place are two determining elements.
>
> Ibid, page 98.

We should not doubt that many of the views that have
guided us thus far are not sufficient for managing social affairs. We must achieve a new vision and understanding.
Relying on current religious leadership is necessary but not
sufficient.

If this central problem is overshadowed by peripheral matters, society will be held back from achieving a desirable solution to problems. Serious as these problems are, we cannot lose our hope in the future. Most important, our young intellectuals must maintain an active and hopeful presence on the social stage.

The late Imam was an irreplaceable blessing for our revolution and the establishment of the Islamic Republic. His legacy remains a great reviver of God's religion in our time. His main difference with other religious revivers is the central leadership role he played in the establishment of Islamic government. He was aware that if religious leaders, thinkers, and intellectuals are not confronted with practical problems, they will not think of solutions. But when Islam came to the political scene, established a government, and took power into its own hands, it confronted the necessity of fulfilling the rational expectations of all people who had put their hopes in the revolution. This encounter was a great step toward the establishment of a new system of thoughts, values, and skills appropriate for our time and place, capable of addressing human needs within an Islamic framework.

The Imam's greatest legacy is indeed the establishment of Islamic government, which has managed to stand despite many pressures and conspiracies against it. The enemies may have hoped that after the Imam's passing away, the system's pillars would unravel. But with the grace of God this did not happen. The institutionalization of leadership after the Imam and our continuing in his path of revolutionary struggle are a source of great hope to us all.

Another source of hope is the current condition of humankind in our era. Our Islamic revolution has raised a storm across the Islamic world and among all of the world's downtrodden. Thus, the utopian yearnings and explosive power latent in the hearts of the world's dispossessed greatly buttress our revolution. If we understand this force and use it effectively, we will be able to confront the opponent despite its economic, military, and political predominance. If we rely on the utopian visions that our revolution has awakened throughout the Islamic world and beyond, and believe that backers of our revolution are ready to sacrifice for it, victory is within our reach.

What adds further hope to our future is that our opponent — despite all its apparent might — has gotten old and is approaching the end of its line. The existence of crisis in the thought and civilization of the West betrays its senility.

Again, our main problem is the fundamental opposition of the values of our revolution to what is dominant in the world on the one hand, and our lack of practical experience in installing a real religious government on the other. What must we do to solve this problem so that with the help of God we can ensure that this revolution remains immune to serious threats?

The unsophisticated among us may opt for the simplistic option of censorship and preventing the values and thoughts of our opponent from reaching and subverting our people. But is this a viable solution?

The low capacity and truncated vision of some may lead them to attack all that does not fit into their closed minds and match their tastes as being against Islam, the revolution, and the legacy of the revolution's martyrs. Unfortunately, there are camps in our society, which, although bereft of proper logic, think of themselves as the pillars of the revolution and Islam, and accuse their opponents of being against Islam and the revolution, as they try to oust their opponents from the political ring at any cost.

But what exactly is the yardstick for judging what is acceptable and what is not? In opposing difficulties and the enemy, what strategy should we adopt? Will our cultural policy be one of censorship and restricting access to all sources we disagree with? Can a policy of isolation from the international community succeed in today's world?

Throughout its glorious history, Islam has never accepted isolation and restricting access as a viable policy. In certain periods this has been imposed on people in the name of Islam, causing irreparable damage, but it has not lasted. Islam has embraced opposing views with open arms. Seminal Muslim thinkers have actively sought to encounter others' views, adopting the good, rejecting or transforming the bad. This openness has imbued Islamic civilization with much intellectual weight.

At the same time, restriction is not practical in today's world. Information channels accessible to our people are not limited to government-run sources. Let us assume that we prevent all faulty prose from being published, stop all newspapers or magazines from printing the smallest bit that offends our tastes, or disallow the production of any films that we find defective. Will these thoughts and views that have been officially banned find no other channel of reaching our people?

In judging what is good and bad in the world of ideas, rigid fixations and dogma may replace strong logic and realistic appraisals much to our detriment. It is naive to think that government-run channels are people's only source of access to international and inter-societal communication.

Today, the global broadcast of mass-communicated electronic images and vibes is under no government's control. How can we prevent dynamic and curious minds from accessing what they desire? How can we build a wall between such minds and the outside world? With the rapid advance of communication technology that is becoming accessible to ever-larger segments of our population, controlling the spread of mass-mediated images will only be more unrealistic and impractical in the future.

Of course, this does not mean that our Islamic system should impose no limitations and restrictions on people's access to information. That would be unrealistic as well. No form of governance can exist without imposing some restrictions, and even the most developed liberal-democracies are not exempt from this rule. But there is a difference between a system that relies on restriction as its main strategy and a system that uses restriction occasionally to tactically deal with sensitive and vital matters. Any system is bound to impose some form of restriction when its whole existence and the fundamentals of its rule are endangered. However, on the whole, Islam has not historically based its system on a policy of restriction and censorship.

The cultural strategy of a dynamic, vibrant Islamic society cannot be isolation. As a progressive religion Islam shuns building fences around people's consciousness. Instead, our strategy must focus on making our people immune, raising and educating them to resist the cultural onslaught of the West on their own. Only a strategy of immunization represents a viable solution for today and tomorrow. This requires us to allow various, disparate views to engage one another in our society. How is it possible to make the body immune without injecting with a controlled and weakened virus, so that it can resist the more extensive and threatening invasion of that virus? The way to make the body resistant to viruses is certainly not preventing any viruses from coming near it. Instead, we must see to it that the living organism has the apparatus to resist the virus itself. In society, too, it cannot be any other way. An active, evolving society must be in contact and communication with different, sometimes opposing views, to be able to equip itself with a more powerful, attractive and effective thought than that of the opponent. And if the sources of revolutionary and religious thought really wish to preserve the revolutionary system, they have no other choice than to offer society sophisticated and adaptive thinking.

At the outset of the revolution, the Imam (Khomeini) counseled against shutting out all that we found undesirable.

And we are proud that our revolution took its first steps on the basis of liberty. This was not an unintended consequence of the revolution, out of our leaders' hands. The principle from the beginning was that others can speak their minds, unless they are engaging in conspiracy. If there were groups who did not want to wisely and fairly use this freedom, abusing and subverting it instead, they were the ones at fault, not the revolution. Society suffered great harm as a result of their unseemly actions. It was the abusers of liberty who did not uphold the supremacy of thought and rationality as they tried to pollute the atmosphere of openness and use it for imposing their autocratic wishes. They did not realize that a government held up by the will and belief of a people and watered by the blood of martyrs and the effort of millions of selfless devotees will stand firm against conspiracy. The limit of legal opposition was conspiracy then and it must be the same today.

The idea of what exactly constitutes conspiracy must be clarified as well. We must look at social problems with a comprehensive and open view. Otherwise any closed-minded and dogmatic person can use the excuse of conspiracy to oust her opponents from the political stage. Our system needs accountability and discipline.

Reckless, half-baked and superficial but politically charged ideas of certain groups can neither determine society's best interests, nor understand conspiracy and its limits. Otherwise, anyone can mount an attack on thoughts different from his own limited tastes with the excuse of defending the interests of the country, the revolution and religion against conspiracy.

Thus, to solve our fundamental problems, we should build and offer superior thinking and logic, as well as more attractive solutions to society's woes. Only in this way can we give hope to the revolution's devotees, adding to their material and spiritual well being. We must endeavor to build a system so solidly grounded that it can not only resist unraveling at the encounter of other systems but can display its vigor and superiority. This impetus to self-affirmation has protected and enriched Islamic thought and the essence of religious belief over the ages.

A system like ours, based as it is on Islamic utopian ideology, is bound to restrict some individual liberties. A revolutionary religious system will naturally forbid much that is accessible to people — particularly the youth — in the West. The overflowing urges of the youth are better satisfied in the West, and hedonistic instincts are fulfilled to a greater degree; whereas in an Islamic system, a multitude of religious rules stand in the way. To make our society stable and strong we must teach the young a more worthy path than hedonism, such that they gain pleasure out of abstinence.

Utopian visions can keep people, especially the youth, confident and lively. Muslim youths must believe that alongside the limitations and restrictions that our system has imposed, it has given them character, imbuing their lives with direction, in whose shadow they feel pride, greatness and tranquillity. Emotional and mental needs must be addressed for people to feel content. If the Islam we offer fails to accomplish this, the foundations of our society will be unstable.

Fulfilling the utopian vision of the revolution's devotees inside and outside Iran is a pressing necessity to ensure our survival. To assert our identity it is necessary to be present in all world forums and to effectively defend Islam and Iran in all international tribunals and conventions. But we cannot ultimately flourish and make our weight felt in the international scene — whose rules are set by our opponents — unless we maintain our unique idealism. Why was it that we had less pressing cultural problems during the eight-year war with Iraq? Because a massive wave of revolutionary youths were at the front lines and people saw themselves as defenders of the revolution and the country. This active presence filled people with deep pride. Our youth felt that their lives had assumed new meaning, and that they had achieved spiritual growth with which they could stand against oppressors and tyrants. Now that the war is over, what must replace it? The only effective solution is preparing the ground for the active involvement of the young generation in all areas where their talents can develop and be put to productive use. If the young generation do not feel active and instrumental in society, it is natural that they feel dejected.

To make society vigorous, thinkers must see in Islam a system of superior logic and ingenious solutions. At the same time, all social forces must be active in the social and political process. Here the greatest mission of intellectuals is to understand real Islam, the kind that our revolution drew from to succeed.

We live in a world that in many ways is at odds with our Islamic revolution's orientation. Opponents continue to conspire. And we want to organize our lives on the basis of Islam. It is necessary to find out exactly what sort of Islam we want to base our lives on. Here, it is incumbent upon our seminaries and universities to answer this question. It is not as though there is no divergence of opinion on what Islam is. Over the past century, if not all of Islamic history, we have confronted three separate Islams. To decide what sort of Islam we want, we must stay clear of factional squabbles such that we can chart our future path on the basis of the right sort of Islam.

Traditionally, we have encountered a regressive, a diluted, and a real Islam. Which of these three was our revolution based on, and which one can save our society and bring honor and pride to it? We believe that the basis of our revolution is the real Islam, the same Islam that has roots in revelation and solid monotheistic perspectives — an Islam that believes in the inherent dignity of humans and wants enlightened happiness for humanity, a constantly evolving Islam that can find solutions to new puzzles as they emerge. All throughout history, this interpretation of Islam has defended against sacrilege and corruption, but it has never been given the opportunity to assert itself in the socio-political sphere.

It is imprudent to assume that since our revolution has succeeded and an Islamic Republic established, the victory of real Islam will be assured automatically. No, we face serious difficulties and dangers. But in the first instance, the devotees of real Islam must equip themselves with rationality, thought

and logic more than ever before. The battle of ideas is a far
more fateful and determining than political and military conflict. First, we have to see which Islam we have accepted and
why. Only then will we muster sufficient moral and intellectual weight to confront our opponents. The experience of our
revolution has taught us invaluable lessons that we cannot
forget.

From the first days that the Imam (Khomeini) took
center stage, he began his religiously inspired struggle against
tyranny, dependency, corruption, cultural degradation, and
American imperialism. Within the ranks of the educated and
senior clergy, there were those who opposed the Imam's
method of struggle and his interpretation of Islam. Some were
sympathizers of the monarchy; others were driven by profit-
seeking, and self-serving motives. Most such people were not
traitors but had an interpretation of Islam that did not suit
the revolution. There were others who supported the Imam
in the initial steps but backed away from supporting him
when matters got more serious.

Many of those devoted to the Imam had endured im-
prisonment and exile to see the revolution through. These
were and are good, dedicated people, but subsequently, when
the time came to institutionalize the revolution, their view of
Islam strayed from the Imam's.

In many cases after the revolution, when the issue of
social justice and combating inequality was voiced, some
screamed that Islam was in danger. I not am saying that all
those who used the slogans of social justice and fighting ine-

quality were on the right path. The issue here is the principle of social justice itself and that there were those who did not even want to bring it up, resisting all practical steps that we wanted to take to ameliorate the problem. Such people could not tolerate the fact that the Imam's Islam wanted social justice, and thus subverted all efforts in this direction. The Imam was compelled to bluntly confront this thinking, stating that on the basis of the Islam he had introduced, achieving social justice was among the primary goals of the revolution.

And there were those who felt that the place of women was the home, arguing that the presence of women in the workplace leads to corruption and moral decay. They were against higher education for women, and opposed women's involvement in social affairs. This was another view that was introduced under the guise of Islam. At the end of the first elected Majles (Parliament) after the revolution, a few influential circles tried to convince the Imam that women should not be allowed to run for seats in the Majles. The Imam confronted this thinking resolutely and defended women's right to take part in the elections. Or there were those who claimed that no one other than the clergy should be allowed to take part in politics. They were especially suspicious of university students and academics, labeling them "deviant" just because they carried intellectual weight. They forbade a large part of society from being involved in the their own political destiny. They would try to justify all this in the name of Islam. Once again, the Imam responded swiftly, scolding their regressive prescriptions.

Some criticized all social and cultural programs to the point of forcing the Imam to explicitly outline the benefits of cultural activities to dispel any doubts. Others were opposed to all music, film and theater. They were not against only some forms of art, but all artistic expression in general. Some even opposed broadcasting sporting events on television and thought it sinful. The Imam confronted all these restrictive and regressive religious views head-on, claiming that much of what they objected to was actually beneficial to society. In the last years of his prolific life, the Imam put forth the most penetrating critique of religious dogma:

> We must endeavor to break the chains of ignorance and superstition to reach the prophet's fresh fountain. Today the most puzzling thing to people is this Islam, and its rescue requires sacrifice; pray that I am myself one of these sacrifices.
>
> Ibid, page 41.

All who truly believe in the revolution and wish to dignify Islam will choose the Islam articulated by the Imam. This should not be taken to mean that others do not have the right to publicly express their views. Everyone is entitled to voice his opinion within the law and the bounds of rationality. However, we must know which interpretation of Islam our revolution is based on. Do the groups that our Imam numerously scolded have the right to impose their extreme views on the people and to portray their opponents as being against Islam and the revolution?

Regressive and dogmatic clerics, those whom the Imam singled out as the greatest danger to the revolution, are not sitting idly by. The enlightened and truly devoted must be mindful of the danger they pose and guard against it.

Alongside the regressive version of Islam, we have the camp that believes in a diluted Islam, a fabricated, inauthentic form of the faith that merely goes through the motions of piety without any real knowledge of Islam or real belief in its teachings. Their Islam has so many foreign, imported elements that it cannot be called Islam at all. Diluted Islam represents one of the most dangerous pores for the West's cultural onslaught. Un-Islamic or anti-Islamic political currents have never enjoyed a popular base and they have never been viewed as the main danger. But those who have had the appearance of piety and have appeared in society with ideas borrowed from the West or others have been able to propagate their views in parts of society.

Opposed to these regressive and diluted views of Islam, we must recognize the real Islam, and the secret of our survival and success is the understanding and implementation of this kind of Islam, in whose shadow we can pass safely through dangers that threaten the existence and health of the revolution and our society. This is the same Islam that the late Imam epitomized, and for which a great mind like Motahhari[1] was martyred. We must discover the target of the

---

[1] Translator's note. Morteza Motahhari (1919–1979). Iranian thinker and cleric who was instrumental in reconciling traditional seminaries with universities. His writings made traditional Islamic con-

Imam's pronouncements, particularly in the last years of his life. A bit of focus will show that the Imam's criticism was directed at those views of Islam that hinder progress and development, paralyzing the search for solutions to difficulties that face our society.

If diluted Islam martyred Motahhari, then regressive Islam has tried to negate the substance of his thought. The confrontations that have been directed at the likes of Motahhari and Beheshti[2] in our society are alarming and serious. And we even witnessed how unseemly this current was to Hashemi-Rafsanjani[3] when he brought up the issue of social justice. To know the real Islam and to base our society upon

---

cepts and the relationship between Iran and Islam accessible to his contemporaries. He was assassinated by armed opponents of the Islamic Republic a few months after the revolution.

[2] Translator's note. Mohammad Hosseini-Beheshti (1921–1980). A cleric and leading ideologue of Iran's Islamic revolution who was assassinated along with scores of other political figures when a bomb exploded in the headquarters of the Islamic Republican Party.

[3] Translator's note. Ali-Akbar Hashemi-Rafsanjani (b.1933). A cleric and political leader in the Islamic Republic of Iran who has served in a number of senior posts culminating in his tenure as President of the Islamic Republic of Iran from 1989 to 1997. In 1997, he was appointed as chairman of the Expediency Council, a high-ranking consultative body.

it, our greatest source of inspiration is the religious and devoted youth in our seminaries and universities. Aided by the knowledge and piety of eminent clergy, we must breed a cadre of new clergy who are up-to-date, aware and enlightened, and we must tirelessly march toward understanding the specific vision of Islam that is the basis of our revolution. It is understanding and explaining this Islam that will make us immune to other schools of thought.

CHAPTER THREE

Observations on the Information World

Much has been said in our era about the central role of information in shaping human destiny, making it possible even to claim that information has surpassed military and political might as the main source of power in today's world. All peoples who seek pride, power and progress must learn to effectively manage this vital resource, staying abreast of constantly evolving communication technologies.

Timely access to information and effective means of disseminating it are central to the development process in every country. We cannot afford to fall farther behind in this rapidly advancing field and must cooperate to effectively produce, store and disseminate information. This is no easy feat.

Most inquiry into the information world focuses exclusively on its technical underpinnings at the expense of exploring its human, political dimension. This task is crucial to our destiny.

In its contemporary, complex forms, information technology represents one of the highest achievements of modern culture which uses its control over information to solidify its domination of the world. Thus, inquiry into the nature of the information world is inseparable from uncovering the nature of modern civilization itself. And until we address this important question we will not be able to muster the confidence and wisdom to understand our relationship to modern civilization. Otherwise, we will live in a world whose rules have been set by others, at the mercy of circumstance, not as masters of our fate.

We confront the Western-dominated information world on two fronts: the realm of scientific information, and the realm of information that has socio-political and cultural significance. In the first case, the scientific method is unanimously regarded as the most authoritative way of understanding the world.

Science has spurred great transformations in human life, and no nation or people can survive without its blessings. Scientific underdevelopment and falling behind the era's technological breakthroughs have a pitiful effect. Yet, the globally preeminent importance of science should not prevent us from asking fundamental questions about the human context of the scientific and technological enterprise. We cannot deify and worship science as though it were beyond the purview of human judgments.

Inquiring into the nature of modern science is especially necessary for us Muslims, who once had seminal, world-class scientists but are now behind the West in this sphere. We have been relegated to being passive consumers of the West's modern civilization. But if we use our rationality and wisdom, we will have the opportunity to break out of our current second-rate status, and we will be able to affect the course of human destiny.

In the eighteenth century, Westerners embraced the magic of science and technology. Grand theorists such as Kant designed their metaphysical systems to match the tenets of the physical sciences. Yet, despite the optimism of eighteenth-century Europeans, people have come to realize that science is incapable of solving a broad range of problems that fall outside its purview.

Today, even the most loyal advocates of modern culture — and the socioeconomic and political system that it has given rise to — think of science as a series of tentative conjectures that constantly await falsification by newer, more complete theories. No one has the last word in the realm of science, for science is nothing more than what scientists perceive and perform. There is no way of knowing for certain that the subjective judgments of scientists accurately depict reality. Today, the objectivity of science has been brought into question more than ever before.

It is true that science has demonstrated remarkable effectiveness in solving practical puzzles, and there is no choice but to use its techniques of trial and error. Still, despite the optimism of eighteenth-century Europeans, we cannot base the whole social order on the institution of modern science which is impotent in addressing the metaphysical, philosophical and mystical yearnings of humans.

Of course, our concerns with the limitations of science do not imply that we must return to the Middle Ages. Nor can we regress to the limited and backward views of religion and spirituality prevalent in those times. Modern humans need new interpretations of spirituality and supernatural phenomena to imbue their lives with meaning. Because of the central place of science and technology in Western civilization, uncertainty about their meaning has led to a general crisis in the West.

This crisis is more acutely felt in the human sciences than in the physical or natural sciences. Modern civilization is more deeply tied to political, cultural, and economic ideas than to the natural sciences. In the human sciences the subject and object of study are the same as humans study themselves, their societies and their political systems. Inquiry is based on the motives and assumptions of the agent or the scientist, not on objective reality. And the identity crisis of the scientific community will naturally permeate the cultural and political sphere.

The flood of information in our age saturates the senses of all humanity so extensively that the ability to assess and choose is impaired even among Westerners who are producers of information, let alone us who have played a peripheral role in the information world. Electronic information is the brainchild of modern civilization. Thus, the power of today's information — based mass culture is tied to the legitimacy of the values of Western civilization for which the information revolution counts as the most prominent achievement.

For those of us outside the West, the information world poses manifold challenges. Today, information is used by advanced industrial countries as the main tool of safeguarding their own economic and political interests, even if they are irreconcilable with the interests of the majority of the world's peoples who live outside the sphere of modern civilization.

Thus, however optimistic some might feel about the benefits of the information revolution for all humanity, we cannot doubt that politically and culturally loaded information is manufactured to protect the interests of industrialized powers while appropriating the rights of deprived and subjugated peoples. As consumers of such information, we cannot ignore that the political will behind information production and dissemination is based on maintaining Western supremacy. Non-Westerners are taught to respect Western supremacy as legitimate, even desirable. Western civilization has used and continues to use all its resources to dominate the minds and lives of all peoples through controlling the sources of information and the means of communication.

This does not mean that we must isolate ourselves from the Western-dominated information world. Such a thing is undesirable and practically impossible as the global reach of information constantly expands. Awareness of today's world events is an imperative for understanding our place in the world and planning our future in it. Being isolated from the world's information networks can only turn us into pawns of others because it is they who control the flow of this vital and strategic resource.

We must reach a level of historical evolution and social maturity to be able to accurately judge the thoughts and efforts of others so that we know our place in the world and can put our own house in order. This way we can choose what benefits us in the new world and reject all that does not. Thus, we must become active on three fronts.

First, we must understand the peculiarities of our era and treat Western civilization as our era's ultimate manifestation and symbol. This means understanding the values and tenets of Western civilization and freeing ourselves from the equally harmful extremes of either hating it or being completely taken in and entranced by it. Second, we must try to come to grips with our own historical identity which has brought many valuable gifts to humanity but has also encountered many difficulties and inadequacies. And third, while we must pay attention to problems that threaten our society from the outside — the hegemonic nature of Western politics, economics and culture — we must also focus on our own internal problems and frictions.

Many of our traditions are human constructs that, however great they might have been in their own time, belong to a different historical epoch and place but have nonetheless maintained the veneer of sanctity and infallibility. Today, dogmatic attachment to archaic ideas poses a serious obstacle to our society, preventing it from utilizing the human achievements and thoughts of our era. Let us not forget that not just the natural world, but religion must also be scrutinized by reflection, for our interpretation of religion is constantly being modified as well.

Our attachment to the past should not mean negating all the achievements of modern, Western civilization. We will not return to the past to stay there, but merely to understand and regain our identity that has been rendered fragile by the onslaught of Western culture. With knowledge and will we can shape the future, which beckons the cooperation and coordination of all devotees and thinkers of the Muslim world. We Muslims have a grand historical legacy that we must revive in today's world.

Despite disagreements among sects within the Islamic world, the unity and coordination of Islamic thought across various parts of the Islamic world has been phenomenal. Over centuries of Islamic history, Andalusian theologians preached in Damascus and Baghdad, just as Persian philosophers and mathematicians felt at home in Africa and Mesopotamia. We Muslims possess the foundations for a solid unity that can create a powerful cultural movement in the future.

First, we possess a common historical bond and system of values that Islam, as the source of a great civilization, has provided us. Although this civilization is no longer globally dominant as it once was, it represents the greatest source of shared experience among all Muslims. Our attachment to the theism of Islam, based on a belief in the unity of God, is the linchpin of the bond that ties all Muslims together.

Second, the increasing awareness of all peoples, especially in this century, has instilled a sense of unity of purpose among Muslims as we all perceive ourselves as the victims of colonialism in its various forms. There is no one among us who has not seen his dignity, freedom and independence violated by colonial powers. We all wish independence and freedom from the shackles of this domination. If we combine our common pains and unify our visions and beliefs, we will sow the seeds of betterment and prosperity in our societies. Shar-

ing and coordinating our information resources represents the
hallmark of this cooperation.

The Islamic Republic of Iran, despite its many differences with the globally dominant political order, has always
championed deep cultural and scientific ties among Muslims
of all countries. And today, we also believe that despite political differences the conditions must be created for the scientists
and thinkers of the whole Muslim world to work together.
All Muslims must firmly join hands to further the cause of
development in their societies.

Covenant with the Nation

Inaugural Speech by

President Seyyed Mohammad Khatami

at the
Islamic Consultative Assembly (*Majles*)
August 4, 1997

In the name of God,
the Compassionate, the Merciful

With the grace and benevolence of God Almighty, and relying upon His omnipotence, here in the House of the Nation, and in the presence of the honorable heads of the Legislature and the Judiciary, members of the Council of Guardians, members of the Assembly of Experts, representatives of the Islamic Consultative Assembly, respected scholars, thinkers and government officials, distinguished Iranian and foreign guests and in front of all my noble Iranian sisters and brothers, I would like to bring to your august attention a number of observations with respect to the heavy responsibility being entrusted, as of today, to this humble servant.

Fulfillment of the obligation to serve the Islamic Republic, the concrete embodiment of a popular revolution, is indeed a great honor. Endeavors towards safeguarding this system and further advancing its stature and authority, as well as the betterment of the spiritual and material life of the courageous people of Iran, constitute an important responsibility for all those committed to Islam, the Revolution and Iran.

The noble people of Iran, through their great, conscientious and discerning presence and participation in the seventh presidential elections, created an epic of historical proportions, thus exhibiting their trust and confidence in their cherished system of governance. Now, the popularly elected Executive branch, along with the other two branches of government, carries heavy responsibilities in response to such a popular and national trust and expectation. The framework and the outline for this heavy responsibility is defined in the Constitution. The Constitution, the covenant of our Islamic and national solidarity, the actual embodiment of popular allegiance to the Islamic Revolution and the great ideals of the late Imam Khomeini, and the document paid for with the blood of our noble martyrs including [President] Rajaie and [Premier] Bahonar, serves as the fundamental reference for the powers and responsibilities of the government and the rights and duties of citizens. Therefore, to serve the people, it is incumbent upon the Executive, and is likewise the mandate and mission of the President of the Islamic Republic, to endeavor towards institutionalizing the rule of law, and the Constitution, first and foremost.

This is the only way the continuity of the Revolution, the dynamism of the system and the power and dignity of the noble people of Iran can be ensured. Hence, our honorable people, led by His Eminence Ayatollah Khamenei, can witness the establishment and preservation of the institutions emanating from the Revolution within the framework of a strong and vibrant society and a stable and law-based structure.

At this juncture, at the beginning of a new phase in the administration of the country and in pursuance of the valuable and admirable efforts of Hojjatol-Eslam Hashemi-Rafsanjani — whose legacy of deeds, ideas and experience will continue to be a great asset for us all — the new government, hoping to draw upon the precious accomplishments of previous administrations during the periods of sacred defense and reconstruction, assumes great responsibilities.

Within the framework of such a responsibility, and before the Holy Qur'an as well as in your august presence, I took the oath to perform the duties which, according to the law, are entrusted to the President:

* Safeguarding the official religion, the Islamic Republic and the Constitution;
* Serving the people and national progress and elevation;
* Promotion of religion and morality;
* Upholding righteousness and promoting justice;
* Desisting from autocracy;
* Protecting the freedom and dignity of individuals and the rights of the nation;
* Safeguarding the territorial integrity and political, economic and cultural independence of the country;
* Holding power as a sacred trust from the people and passing it on to the next elected President.

This oath is a religiously binding commitment. As defined in Islam, such oaths or vows must be taken with the purest intentions and with the intent and resolve to fulfill them. And the person taking the oath must, in potential and deed, be capable of fulfilling his religious undertaking.

The responsibilities enumerated in the presidential oath refer to social duties. Hence, with respect to collective responsibilities, the individual assumes undertakings whose fulfillment goes far beyond his individual capabilities. And as such, it is only public resolve and national solidarity that can make the performance of such heavy undertakings possible.

The epic participation of the noble and discerning people of Iran in this round of elections encourages me to claim that the entire nation has joined hands in unison for the fulfillment of the provisions and commitments of this oath, and intends to lay the foundations for a better tomorrow for Islamic Iran. Such a will and resolve on the part of the people and the authorities, to help the government while monitoring and overseeing its performance in action, is indeed a great asset and will certainly serve to facilitate the fulfillment of official responsibilities as well as mutual duties and obligations of government and the people.

On governance and the relations between the ruler and the ruled, Imam Ali (peace be upon him) directs the people to the following:

* Do not praise me, so that I can fulfill the rights that are left unrealized and perform the obligations that are left undone.
* Do not address me the way despots are addressed, and do not avoid me as the ill-tempered are treated.
* Do not approach me with an air of artificiality, and do not think that I find the truth offensive.
* I do not want you to revere me.
* He who finds listening to complaints difficult will surely find administration of justice even more so.

* Therefore, do not hesitate in telling the truth or in advising me on matters of justice.
* I am neither above fallibility nor am I immune from error in my conduct, unless God safeguards me from the self, over which He commands more control than I.

Such being the case in the eyes of Imam Ali (peace be upon him), the infallible exemplar of justice of all times, undoubtedly it is much more difficult for common human beings like us. Therefore, towards the fulfillment of the commitments that lie beyond individual capability or even that of the government by itself, I seek guidance and grace from God Almighty and help and support from the noble people of Iran.

The Leadership, with his unique position in the system and society, and his supervision of the three branches of government, will undoubtedly guide and assist us in performing these duties. Likewise, the esteemed senior religious scholars and jurisprudents will assist the government in serving the people with their kind counsel and prayers.

I seek assistance from the Islamic Consultative Assembly, which embodies the virtues of the nation and constitutes the body to legislate and supervise the implementation of laws. Through exercising their legal duty to supervise the performance and conduct of government institutions and authorities and by presenting useful and constructive suggestions, distinguished members of parliament can contribute to the welfare of the nation and more efficient administration of the country, and thus achieve God's blessings and salvation.

I expect the honorable Judiciary to assist the Executive branch in the management of a safe, secure and just society founded on the rule of law.

I also call on political institutions and organizations, associations, the media, scholars and researchers, academicians and educators, experts and specialists, all men and women of science, letters, culture and art, and all citizens in all walks of life to help us with their continuous supervision and candid presentation of their demands and views. I call on all to increase the extent of public participation in national policy-making at the macro level through continuous evaluation and critique of programs, policies and performances. Certainly, a higher level of involvement and participation by experts in the process of government policy-making not only facilitates the fulfillment of mutual duties and obligations of the government and the people, but is also conducive to the realization of the people's most fundamental right, the right to determine their own destiny.

To attain this objective, the government is obligated to provide a safe environment for the exchange of ideas and views within the framework of the criteria set by Islam and the Constitution. The government must promote the culture and capacity for participation, evaluation, critique and reform. It must itself be the model for tolerance and take the lead in empowerment of the people for participation. For the realization of these objectives, God-willing, the main thrust of the overall policies of the Executive branch will be based on:

* Institutionalizing the rule of law;
* Vigorous pursuit of justice as an exalted religious value and the pivotal factor for social trust, stability, progress and prosperity;
* Promoting and consolidating the principle of accountability which will improve performance while facilitating the intellectual, political and social advancement of the population;
* Empowering the people in order to achieve and ensure an ever-increasing level of their discerning participation.

It is my hope that this great responsibility will be successfully fulfilled through popular participation and coordination among the three branches of government. The government's belief in the necessity of promoting and consolidating the rule of law in individual and social interactions will in itself expand the possibilities for a higher level of coordination among the Executive, the Legislature and the Judiciary.

When the government relies on the law in order to serve the people and ensure their participation on a continuous basis, and simultaneously the Legislature is committed to the execution of its paramount role of legal monitoring and supervision of the country's administration, the development of a proper political structure in the society may be attained.

Therefore, establishment of the rule of law is an Islamic, revolutionary and national obligation, and an absolute imperative, which requires a conducive and enabling envi-

ronment as well as legal means and instruments coupled with
public involvement and assistance.

Out of deep conviction in such a necessity, I presented
a program upon entering the presidential campaign which I
expected to form the basis of the people's understanding, appraisal and support, and hopefully eventually, the covenant
between the President and the nation. The outline and the essence of my program was inspired by the provisions of the
oath I just took. Our honorable people's vote in this election,
a vote for the proposed program, has further underlined the
necessity of serious attention to these concepts and elements
and more importantly, their implementation.

The Constitution obligates the President with:

*   Safeguarding the official religion, the Islamic Republic
    and the Constitution;
*   Promoting religion and morality;
*   Upholding righteousness and the promotion of justice.

This is a clear indication of the paramount importance
and priority of religion and spirituality in our system. The Islamic revolution is an invitation to the revival of monotheistic thinking and the preponderance of Islamic belief and conduct. It is indeed our unique honor that such a great revolution with far-reaching dimensions and implications was led to
victory by a Mujahid jurisprudent, a revolutionary mystic,
and a statesman immersed in moral virtues.

Ever since its establishment, the Government of the Islamic Republic of Iran has always felt duty-bound to base its programs and policies on the essence and objectives of Islam, to ensure their compatibility with religious norms and edicts, to prepare the necessary grounds for the promotion of Islamic thinking and spirituality, to eliminate moral decadence and vice from society, and to conduct all executive planning and policy-making with the spirit of justice. The pertinent institutions of the Islamic Republic have been active in promoting the observance of religious norms and precepts.

It should be borne in mind, however, that in practice only through internalized perpetuation of divine values can the individual and society attain salvation.

To this end, the criteria and yardsticks for ethics and behavior, and for social relations and conduct, should be the same values and teachings the Holy Prophet of Islam (peace be upon him) has received through revelation and relayed to humankind. Hence, as indicated by the late Imam Khomeini, we should always consider the elements of time and place in the question of Islamic *Ijtihad* [independent interpretation of Islamic jurisprudence] and understand Islam in such a manner that it can respond to and meet emerging issues and needs of all times. We should all avoid considering our own understandings and interpretations as absolute, which can only be attributed to the Book and the Divine Revelation itself.

Under the Islamic system, justice and the welfare of mankind should prevail. To this end, reason and intellect are to be utilized. The best way for the establishment of justice lies in utilizing the best of research and expertise. It is only through the growth of thinking and intellectual forces in society, and the free exchange of ideas, that the government can choose the best views and ways and arrive at the proper criteria for justice in the sophisticated world of today, given the complex mechanisms governing economic, political and cultural relations in society.

A morally and materially prosperous individual and society who find the Islamic system capable of providing for their reasonable needs, and protecting their rights and dignity, will develop more devotion and commitment, and this constitutes the single best and most principled way for the promotion of religion. A society that enjoys material and spiritual blessings is the one that reflects the truly attractive image of Islam and the revolution; such a society can indeed be a model for emulation in today's world.

For the government to move in this direction, there is no other way but to extend justice and equity to all economic, social and cultural spheres. Creating opportunities and ensuring equal access to possibilities and privileges, providing a conducive environment for the realization of potentials, flourishing the talents of men and women in all spheres, alleviating poverty, and provision of decent living conditions for all, particularly the needy and the underprivileged, are among the most imperative obligations of the Islamic government. To eliminate poverty, the national economy should be made strong and robust.

Hence, what we need most is balanced, sustained and comprehensive development that should be realized in all political, economic, cultural and scientific spheres.

In our view, there is an organic interdependence between development and justice. Development without justice will lead to ever-widening social gaps, while justice without development will lead to the expansion of poverty.

Therefore, our principal need is balanced, sustained and comprehensive development in all spheres. Human resources are central in the development process. As a consequence, safeguarding the dignity of humans, human resource development, advancement of culture, higher education and research in society, as well as provision of proper scientific and technical training, are among the major duties of the government.

Protecting the freedom of individuals and the rights of the nation, which constitute a fundamental obligation of the President upon taking the oath, is an imperative emanating from the exalted worth and dignity of the human person enshrined in our Divine religion. Fulfillment of this responsibility can only be attained through wider popular awareness of their own rights, provision of the necessary conditions for the realization of constitutionally guaranteed liberties, strengthening and expanding the institutions of the civil society, promoting ethics, strengthening the culture of dialogue, discourse, appraisal and critique, and preventing any violation of integrity, dignity and constitutional rights and freedoms of individuals.

Institutionalizing the rule of law and founding social interactions on a legal framework will provide a favorable milieu for the realization of social needs and demands. In a society well acquainted with its own rights and ruled by law, rights and legal constraints of all citizens are recognized and given due attention. In such a society, the state and the people, inter-linked with corresponding rights and obligations, find their respective proper meaning and place. Anybody who lives under the Islamic system and complies with the law is entitled to the rights of life, freedom of expression, enjoyment of a decent living and participation in social, economic and political affairs. The state has a duty to safeguard these rights and boundaries and to provide the people with the necessary milieu and means of tranquillity and peace of mind in all public and private spheres of life, advancing the rule of law and consolidating security and stability.

Serving the people and national progress and elevation, and safeguarding the territorial integrity and the political, economic and cultural independence of the country, constitute other important components of presidential responsibility which emanate from Islamic and human values and which place further obligations upon the Islamic state.

Attention to the living conditions of the people is a paramount principle, vital for the existence and survival of the state. We must believe in the people; we must live with their pain and suffering. Stature of the authorities lies not only in their service to the people but also in considering this to be their primary responsibility. Moreover, strengthening and promoting the spirit of national pride and self-esteem, safeguarding our territorial integrity and national independence, fostering popular vigilance and readiness, and promoting and strengthening the Iranian identity on the basis of Islamic and human values, are among the most pivotal duties of the government.

A proud, prosperous and independent Iran on the world scene is the common aspiration of all devoted and dedicated Iranians. Hence, it is of utmost importance for the government to devote itself to promoting the national interests and prestige of the Islamic Republic, commensurate with her historical, cultural, geographical and economic standing. Safeguarding and protecting the rights of all Iranian nationals all over the world, defending the rights of the world's Muslims and the downtrodden, particularly the oppressed people of Palestine, and active participation in collective endeavors toward universal progress and advancement, while resisting wisely and decisively the expansionist policies of the domineering powers, foreign threats or outside aggression in cultural, political and military fields, are all important duties.

The government must emphasize that in our world, dialogue among civilizations is an absolute imperative. We shall avoid any course of action that may foster tension. We shall have relations with any state which respects our independence. It is our right to make decisions on the basis of national interest. But we shall stand firm against any power who may seek to impose its will on us.

Desisting from autocracy and holding power as a sacred trust are also among the obligations of the President which call attention to the question of the distribution of power in society. The legitimacy of the government stems from the people's vote. And a powerful government, elected by the people, is representative, participatory and accountable. The Islamic government is the servant of the people and not their master, and it is accountable to the nation under all circumstances.

The people must believe that they have the right to determine their own destiny and that the power of the state is bound by limits and constraints set by law. State authority cannot be attained through coercion and dictatorship. Rather, it must be realized through governing according to the law, respecting all rights and obligations, as well as legal constraints on the exercise of power and authority, empowering people to participate and ensuring their involvement in decision-making.

Popular participation requires the emergence of new and divergent expectations. Meeting such expectations, although entailing some difficulty, can be attained through the presence and involvement of the people themselves. In our Islamic and revolutionary society, which enjoys immense and varied material and spiritual resources, and has to its credit, at various levels, great popular epics and accomplishments, meeting such needs and expectations is far from insurmountable.

Meeting society's demands and expectations, making the relations between the Executive apparatus and the people more simple and transparent, and establishing and maintaining the relations between the government and the people on the basis of mutual honesty, trust and confidence, will undoubtedly help to ensure the responsible and participatory presence of the people in the future of our nation. With the help of the Almighty, I will endeavor to direct the Executive branch toward preserving and expanding the existing trend of the presence and participation of the entire populace, and ensuring accountability to the nation which is essential for political development, and hence, for the legitimacy of the state and for sustained comprehensive national development.

Our people are the most precious asset and resource of our state, and their continual presence in all spheres of national administration is an inescapable necessity. It is they who have created epics of victory.

Our contemporary history, from the anti-colonial movements [in the nineteenth century] to the Constitutional Revolution — which we revere and whose anniversary we celebrate today — to the great Islamic Revolution and the Sacred Defense, all bear witness to this fact. It is the people's firm belief and resolute will that has rendered many impossibles possible.

At this new historical chapter in the life of our country, I assert my trust in the Islamic and national will, and in the determination of the entire nation. The vigilance, will, devotion and commitment of all women and men, particularly the youth, give me more hope in the future. I hope that through the grace of God Almighty, national unity, cooperation of all officials and government institutions, and coordination among the Executive, the Legislature and the Judiciary, will help me meet my grave responsibilities and fulfill the provisions of the important oath I just took.

I conclude these words with paying tribute to the memory of our honorable martyrs and a humble homage to the sacrificing war veterans, proud prisoners of war, heroic devotees of the Revolution and the respectable families of them all.

And our last call is that all praise be to God, the Cherisher and Sustainer of the worlds.

Excerpts from Addresses

by

Seyyed Mohammad Khatami

On the Rule of Law

For various cultural and historical reasons, neglecting order and disregarding the law have become habits in our society, because before the revolution, wherever this nation saw any order or law, it was by a power that had imposed itself on this nation by resorting to force and bullying, and there was nothing but contradiction between the interests of the people and the interests of the government. Today, this society is experiencing a government and a system that has arisen from the depths of its own conscience, faith, wishes and interests. That historical mentality [of disregard for the law] must be done away with.

Fighting evasion of the law is a matter to which utmost attention must be paid.

All the rights of the people should be observed. What is important is to bring about social and individual security within the framework of the Constitution.

We hope to gradually witness a more legal society ... with more clearly defined rights and duties for citizens and the government.

Today, our religious, Islamic, revolutionary and national mission dictates that we consolidate society on the basis of the Constitution and institutionalize law in our society, especially because we must complete overnight a road that is one-hundred years long.

The government must take the lead in abiding by the law. A powerful government is one that officially recognizes the rights of the people and the nation within the framework of law and makes every effort to guarantee their rights and lays the groundwork for the implementation of those rights.

****

On Civil Society and Freedom of the Press

To provide channels to convey people's needs to the state, we need organized political parties, social associations, and an independent free press. The government must eliminate obstacles in expansing these institutions.

In this part of the world, and especially in Iran, religion has called people to establish and consolidate civil society, a responsible society, a society in which people are participants, a society where the government belongs to the people and is the servant of the people, not their master, and is consequently responsible to the people. Civil society needs to be based on order and the cornerstone of that order, is the Constitution.

****

On Social Justice

Without a doubt, it is unseemly for this society to see poverty in its midst. Discrimination and injustice are unseemly in our society.

****

On Iran's Strenghts

What we want is a society that is developed, free, proud, wise and virtuous, and such a society is in keeping with the dignity of the great Muslim and revolutionary nation of Iran. We must be brimming with hope for the future. All factors point to such hope for us. The immense resources at our disposal guarantee our success in great tasks, just as they have in the past: a shining record of civilization and culture, the constructive effect of Islam and *velayat* [religious guardianship] in this country, possessing the youngest society in the world [Iran has a high percentage of young people], an outstanding geopolitical position, plentiful resources and vast material reserves, two decades of experience in institutionalizing a new government and success in safeguarding it and in safeguarding independence in all arenas, benefiting from an experienced managerial force that has been through the Sacred Defense [Iran-Iraq war] and the period of reconstruction, and, above all, benefiting from [the support of] all the people, a mass of talented, brave, resilient, informed and self-reliant individuals.

****

On Social Justice

Economic development is not necessarily the same as social justice. Justice has an Islamic and humane value. . . . The principle of justice must always be taken into account in all programs.

To achieve social justice we must create equal opportunities for everyone: creating equal opportunities for all those who have knowledge, ability, talent and want to work. A just and balanced distribution of profits generated by development is necessary . . . the amendment of the taxation system and the appropriate collection of taxes and their correct usage are main steps toward social justice.

Increasing the number and reach of cooperatives as a form of expanding the ownership base, and ensuring people's participation, is a very important measure.

Extending the ownership share of workers and employees in government enterprises and factories is also a way of ensuring economic justice in society. Alongside this, social welfare programs shall be boosted: all different groups and various regions should have access to educational, health and similar facilities.

Assessing the situation of retired people who have used all their strength to serve the nation, we will employ those who may still have the ability to work and provide a good living standard for those who do not have the ability to work anymore.

We cannot afford to tolerate poverty and prejudice in our society. Justice requires that we pay attention to this fact alongside economic growth and development.

****

On Economic Development

We should possess economic independence, an independence that is the product of this revolution and must be consolidated and safeguarded. What is meant by economic independence is that, during the period of construction and development, we will rely on our domestic work force and on our plentiful domestic resources. Of course, shortcomings in domestic resources will be made up for by the use of foreign resources. However, we will rely mainly on our own work force and domestic resources.

In this arena, reliance on production is important. If production becomes extensive and grows in a balanced way in quality and quantity, it will solve many of our problems. Production creates employment. Production will create an equilibrium between supply and demand. Increasing production in the non-oil sectors is of paramount importance.

A structural expansion of industry must be given priority alongside agriculture. Ensuring the profitability of industrial and agricultural products, combating parasitic eco-

nomic activities and unproductive trade, strengthening the
national currency, and increasing foreign exchange reserves
are some efforts that can assist us in the attainment of a vibrant economy.

Development is not limited to economic growth. One can
even say that economic development on its own — without
paying attention to other issues — can be harmful. Uneven
development is tragic. If economic growth is not coupled
with scientific, cultural and political development, we will
not have comprehensive, sustainable and balanced development.

****

On Democratization

Ensuring the active involvement of people in all fields and
trying to strengthen civic foundations, within which individuals and groups identify and defend their rights and find
opportunities to participate in all social spheres, is important.
Organizing society on the basis of law, and institutionalizing
individual and social behaviour on the basis of law is, by itself, a sign of political development.

****

On the Rights of Palestinians

Regarding the so-called Middle East peace process, we believe that there will be no possibility for peace except through the restoration of the legal rights of all Palestinian people.

We are interested in peace and tranquility . . . under the condition that the rights of all sides be observed.

Of course, we are not going to intervene in this matter, and we are going to leave it to the people of Palestine and the governments and people of the region. But we maintain the right to express our views regarding the matter . . . and realistically, we do not think that the current process will come to any satisfactory conclusion.

We believe that there can be no peace until all the legitimate demands of the Palestinian people are met. You cannot talk about peace when the basic rights of Palestinians have been infringed.

****

On Relations with the USA

Our relations with the United States will depend on observing changes in their attitude towards us, but unfortunately we have not seen anything. . . . The key to solving the problem lies in their hands, not in ours.

****

On Terrorism

We have always been against terrorism, especially state-sponsored terrorism. We should join hands to fight terrorism.

****

On Persian Gulf Islands

Our dispute with the United Arab Emirates must be solved through dialogue and negotiation. The interference of other governments or foreign powers is not in the interests of either country.

****

On Foreign Policy

We are in favor of reducing tension throughout the world, especially in our region.

We announce that we are in favor of relations with all countries and nations who respect our independence, dignity and interests.

We are in favor of expanding our relations throughout the world on the basis of the three firm principles of wisdom, dignity and [national] interests.

Under no circumstances shall we compromise with aggressive bullies. Our independence is a principle to us. We have not achieved it at a low price, and we will not relinquish it. In no way shall we allow any power to interfere in our domestic affairs.

We demand the unconditional withdrawal of foreign navies and forces from the region. We believe that the security and advancement of the region should be achieved by the people, nations and governments of the region.

We will not interfere in the affairs of others. We have no intention of doing so, and we have not interfered either.

We are in favor of extensive cooperation with our neighbors, with Muslims and with all independent countries, especially those countries whose position is complementary to our economic and political situation.

The basis of our relations with the other countries is reliance upon the independence and the national interests of our country.

****

Biographical Note

Seyyed Muhammad Khatami was elected President of the Islamic Republic of Iran on May 23, 1997 with over two-thirds of the popular vote. He was born in 1942 into a middle-class clerical family in the town of Ardakan, located in the province of Yazd in central Iran. His father, Grand Ayatollah Ruhollah Khatami, was widely respected for his piety and progressive views.

At the age of nineteen, Khatami left Ardakan to pursue religious studies in Qom until 1965, when he entered the University of Isfahan to study philosophy. From this time onward, he became active in Islamic politics. In 1969, he began graduate studies in education at the University of Tehran. Two years later, he returned to Qom to pursue further religious studies in Islamic law, jurisprudence, and philosophy. It was in Qom that he became more immersed in political actvity. In 1978, on the eve of the Iranian revolution, he was chosen to lead the Hamburg Islamic Institute in Germany, which played a pivotal role in organizing revolutionary activity among the Iranian diaspora. From 1982 to 1992, he served as minister of Culture and Islamic Guidance. During this period he was also briefly head of the War Information Headquarters. In 1992 he was appointed assistant to the President and head of the National Library of Iran, a position he held until his election to the Presidency.

Mr. Khatami is familiar with German, English, and Arabic. He has published two books: *Bim-e Mowj (Fear of the Wave)*, 1993, and *Az Donya-ye Shahr ta Shahr-e Donya (From the City-World to the World-City)*, 1994. He is particualrly interested in the works of Farabi, Molla-Sadra, Sheykh Ansari, and Hafez. He is married and has three children.